M000309766

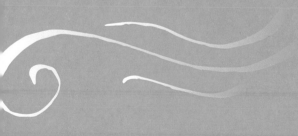

Air

Applewood Books
Carlisle, Massachusetts

978-1-4290-9412-2

To inquire about this edition
or to request a free copy
of our current catalog
featuring our best-selling books, write to:
Applewood Books
P.O. Box 27
Carlisle, MA 01741
For more complete listings,
visit us on the web at:
www.awb.com

10 9 8 7 6 5 4 3 2 1
MANUFACTURED IN THE UNITED STATES OF AMERICA

Air, the invisible element: it surrounds us and fills our senses—a soft wind felt, a sweet breeze smelled, a forceful gale feared—yet it cannot be seen. And, although it cannot be seen, our lives depend upon its presence. The quotations about air in this volume—often poetic—visualize air in many ways: winds of change, the breath of life, open air and adventure, vitality. Together, these quotations show us that air is a multifaceted and potent symbol, and has been throughout the centuries.

The symbol of contentment, the warm breeze can quickly shift and become a chill wind or an unpredictable force. For this reason, air and wind can be used to good effect in both poetry and prose. And novelist Toni Morrison demonstrates this beautifully with this quote from her 1977 novel, *Song of Solomon:* "If you surrender to the air, you can ride it."

Intimately connected with breathing, air has been understood for centuries as the life force, the carrier of vital energy, even spirit. For this reason, you'll find quotations from spiritual leaders, health practitioners, naturalists, and scientists alike. This volume offers a glimpse into the beauty and mystery of air, as expressed by Thich Nhat Hanh, a Vietnamese Buddhist monk and Zen master: "Smile, breathe and go slowly."

—Applewood Books

"When the wind of change blows, some build walls, while others build windows."

—Ancient Chinese proverb

"A wind has blown the rain away and blown the sky away and all the leaves away, and the trees stand. I think, I too, have known autumn too long."

—E. E. Cummings

"Live in the sunshine, swim the sea, Drink the wild air's salubrity."

—Ralph Waldo Emerson

"If you love a flower that lives on a star, it is sweet to look at the sky at night. All the stars are a-bloom with flowers…"

—Antoine de Saint-Exupéry

"Another glorious day, the air as delicious to
the lungs as nectar to the tongue; indeed the
body seems one palate, and tingles equally
throughout."

—John Muir

"The air up there in the clouds is very pure and
fine, bracing and delicious. And why shouldn't it
be?—it is the same the angels breathe."

—Mark Twain

"For me, a landscape does not exist in its own
right, since its appearance changes at every
moment; but the surrounding atmosphere
brings it to life—the light and the air which vary
continually. For me, it is only the surrounding
atmosphere which gives subjects their true value."

—Claude Monet

"Air, air, fresh life-blood, thin and searching air,
The clear, dear breath of God that loveth us.
Where small birds reel and winds take their
delight!"

—Robert Browning

"The natural function of the wing is to soar upwards and carry that which is heavy up to the place where dwells the race of gods. More than any other thing that pertains to the body it partakes of the nature of the divine."

—Plato

"Some old-fashioned things like fresh air and sunshine are hard to beat. In our mad rush for progress and modern improvements let's be sure we take along with us all the old-fashioned things worth while."

—Laura Ingalls Wilder

"O to speed where there is space enough and air enough at last!"

—Walt Whitman

"Kites rise highest against the wind, not with it."

—Winston Churchill

"If you surrender to the air, you can ride it."

—Toni Morrison

"To be one with the wind is to be at home in the World."

—Richard Bode

"Space is the breath of art."

—Frank Lloyd Wright

"Sometimes, flying feels too godlike to be attained by man. Sometimes, the world from above seems too beautiful, too wonderful, too distant for human eyes to see…"

—Charles A. Lindbergh

"So fine was the morning except for a streak of wind here and there that the sea and sky looked all one fabric, as if sails were stuck high up in the sky, or the clouds had dropped down into the sea."

—Virginia Woolf

"Thought is the wind, knowledge the sail, and mankind the vessel."

—Augustus Hare

"There is one way of breathing that is shameful and constricted. Then, there's another way: a breath of love that takes you all the way to infinity."
   —Rumi

"O, thou art fairer than the evening air
Clad in the beauty of a thousand stars."
   —Christopher Marlowe

"Words are easy, like the wind; faithful friends are hard to find…"
   —William Shakespeare

"There is no sport equal to that which aviators enjoy while being carried through the air on great white wings."
   —Wilbur Wright

"Perhaps the wind
Wails so in winter for the summer's dead,
And all sad sounds are nature's funeral cries
For what has been and is not."
   —George Eliot (Mary Ann Evans)

"Sweet life continues in the breeze, in the golden fields."

—Jack Kerouac

"It's remarkable how quickly a good and favorable wind can sweep away the maddening frustrations of shore living."

—Ernest K. Gann

"You haven't seen a tree until you've seen its shadow from the sky."

—Amelia Earhart

"The air to a glider pilot is a reality.... He is trying to understand it in all its moods; to learn its flow, its laws, and to try and use this knowledge to his own ends."

—Philip Wills

"To reach a port we must sail, sometimes with the wind, and sometimes against it. But we must not drift or lie at anchor."

—Oliver Wendell Holmes

"In order to arrive at knowledge of the motions of birds in the air, it is first necessary to acquire knowledge of the winds, which we will prove by the motions of water in itself, and this knowledge will be a step enabling us to arrive at the knowledge of beings that fly between the air and the wind."
—Leonardo da Vinci

"Live in each season as it passes; breathe the air, drink the drink, taste the fruit, and resign yourself to the influence of each."
—Henry David Thoreau

"The answer, my friend, is blowin' in the wind, The answer is blowin' in the wind."
—Bob Dylan

"It's wonderful to climb the liquid mountains of the sky, Behind me and before me is God and I have no fears."
—Helen Keller

"I love to breathe. Oxygen is sexy!"
—Kris Carr

"He lives most life whoever breathes most air."

—Elizabeth Barrett Browning

"People talk of the 'whispering wind.' But what are these secrets of the breeze? I don't know, but I don't want a gossip to stand downwind of me."

—Jarod Kintz

"No one but Night, with tears on her dark face, Watches beside me in this windy place."

—Edna St. Vincent Millay

"I take the paraglider to the mountain or I roll Daisy out of her hangar and I pick the prettiest part of the sky and I melt into the wing and then into the air, till I'm just soul on a sunbeam."

—Richard Bach

"The modern airplane creates a new geographical dimension. A navigable ocean of air blankets the whole surface of the globe. There are no distant places any longer: the world is small and the world is one."

—Wendell Willkie

"Who can feel poor when the sails are full and the spirit is full?"

—Herb Payson

"And 't is my faith, that every flower
Enjoys the air it breathes."

—William Wordsworth

"O, wind,
If Winter comes, can Spring be far behind?"

—Percy Bysshe Shelley

"'Listen to th' wind wutherin' round the house,'
she said. 'You could bare stand up on the moor if
you was out on it tonight.'

   "Mary did not know what 'wutherin' meant
until she listened, and then she understood. It
must mean that hollow shuddering sort of roar
which rushed round and round the house, as
if the giant no one could see were buffeting it
and beating at the walls and windows to try to
break in. But one knew he could not get in, and
somehow it made one feel very safe and warm
inside a room with a red coal fire."

   —Frances Hodgson Burnett

"Every time I have gone up in an aeroplane and
looked down I have realized I was free of the
ground, I have had the consciousness of a new
discovery. 'I see:' I have thought, 'This was the
idea. And now I understand everything.'"

   —Isak Dinesen

"Move swift as the Wind and closely-formed as
the Wood. Attack like the Fire and be still as the
Mountain."

   —Sun Tzu

"Look, up in the sky! It's a bird! It's a plane! It's Superman!"

—Announcer from the "Superman" TV series, 1952

"Our best built certainties are but sand-houses and subject to damage from any wind of doubt that blows."

—Mark Twain

"Most people never run far enough on their first wind to find out they've got a second."

—William James

"The winds have welcomed you with softness,
The sun has greeted you with its warm hands,
You have flown so high and so well,
That God has joined you in laughter,
And set you back gently into
The loving arms of Mother Earth."

—The Balloonist Prayer

"Imagination is the highest kite one can fly."

—Lauren Bacall

"How long can men thrive between walls of brick, walking on asphalt pavements, breathing the fumes of coal and of oil, growing, working, dying, with hardly a thought of wind, and sky, and fields of grain, seeing only machine-made beauty, the mineral-like quality of life?"

—Charles A. Lindbergh

"The wind makes you ache in some place that is deeper than your bones. It may be that it touches something old in the human soul, a chord of race memory that says, Migrate or die— *migrate or die.*"

—Stephen King

"The life of an Indian is like the wings of the air. That is why you notice the hawk knows how to get his prey. The Indian is like that. The hawk swoops down on its prey, so does the Indian. In his lament he is like an animal. For instance, the coyote is sly, so is the Indian. The eagle is the same. That is why the Indian is always feathered up, he is a relative to the wings of the air."

—Black Elk

"The airplane has unveiled for us the true face of the earth."

—Antoine de Saint-Exupéry

"Love is anterior to life, posterior to death, initial of creation, and the exponent of breath."

—Emily Dickinson

"'Excuse me while I kiss the sky."

—Jimi Hendrix

"The higher we soar, the smaller we appear to those who cannot fly."

—Friedrich Nietzsche

"Wind is to us [sailors] what money is to life on shore."

—Sterling Hayden

"I took a deep breath and listened to the old brag of my heart: I am, I am, I am."

—Sylvia Plath

"The wind is a very difficult sound to get. It's always changing."

　　—Captain Beefheart

"What can we do but keep on breathing in and out, modest and willing, and in our places?"

　　—Mary Oliver

"If you reveal your secrets to the wind, you should not blame the wind for revealing them to the trees."

　　—Khalil Gibran

"Trees go wandering forth in all directions with every wind, going and coming like ourselves, traveling with us around the sun two million miles a day, and through space heaven knows how fast and far!"

　　—John Muir

"Feelings come and go like clouds in a windy sky. Conscious breathing is my anchor."

　　—Thich Nhat Hanh

"Who has seen the wind,
Neither you nor I
But when the trees bow down their heads
The wind is passing by."
  —Yoko Ono

"Twenty years from now you will be more
disappointed by the things that you didn't do
than by the ones you did do. So throw off the
bowlines. Sail away from the safe harbor. Catch
the trade winds in your sails. Explore. Dream.
Discover."
  —H. Jackson Brown

"In the love of narrow souls I make many short
voyages but in vain—I find no sea room— but
in great souls I sail before the wind without a
watch, and never reach the shore."
  —Henry David Thoreau

"A boy's will is the wind's will,
And the thoughts of youth are long, long
    thoughts."
  —Henry Wadsworth Longfellow

"I decided to fly through the air and live in the sunlight and enjoy life as much as I could."

—Evel Knievel

"Louisiana in September was like an obscene phone call from nature. The air—moist, sultry, secretive, and far from fresh—felt as if it were being exhaled into one's face. Sometimes it even sounded like heavy breathing. Honeysuckle, swamp flowers, magnolia, and the mystery smell of the river scented the atmosphere, amplifying the intrusion of organic sleaze. It was aphrodisiac and repressive, soft and violent at the same time. In New Orleans, in the French Quarter, miles from the barking lungs of alligators, the air maintained this quality of breath, although here it acquired a tinge of metallic halitosis, due to fumes expelled by tourist buses, trucks delivering Dixie beer, and, on Decatur Street, a mass-transit motor coach named Desire."

—Tom Robbins

"Neither fire nor wind, birth nor death can erase our good deeds."

—Buddha

"Smell is a potent wizard that transports you across thousands of miles and all the years you have lived. The odors of fruits waft me to my southern home, to my childhood frolics in the peach orchard. Other odors, instantaneous and fleeting, cause my heart to dilate joyously or contract with remembered grief. Even as I think of smells, my nose is full of scents that start to awake sweet memories of summers gone and ripening fields far away."

—Helen Keller

"Breathe in the fresh air of the freedom to create your own mood rather than the stale air of being a prisoner of circumstance."

—M. J. Durkin

"The world's a nicer place in my beautiful
    balloon
It wears a nicer face in my beautiful balloon
We can sing a song and sail along the silver sky
For we can fly we can fly
Up, up and away
My beautiful, my beautiful balloon…"

—Jimmy Webb

"A little wind kindles, much puts out the fire."

   —George Herbert

"Our most basic common link is that we all inhabit this planet. We all breathe the same air. We all cherish our children's future. And, we are all mortal."

   —John F. Kennedy

"Every intoxicating delight of early spring was in the air. The breeze that fanned her cheek was laden with subtle perfume and the crisp, fresh odor of unfolding leaves."

   —Gene Stratton-Porter

"Throw your dreams into space like a kite, and you do not know what it will bring back, a new life, a new friend, a new love, a new country."

   —Anaïs Nin

"If one does not know to which port one is sailing, no wind is favorable."

   —Lucius Annaeus Seneca

"Oxygen flooded into the atmosphere as a
pollutant, even a poison, until natural selection
shaped living things to thrive on the stuff and,
indeed, suffocate without it."

—Richard Dawkins

"'I'll stay till the wind changes,' she said
shortly, and she blew out her candle and got
into bed."

—P. L. Travers from *Mary Poppins*

"When all the trees have been cut down, when
all the animals have been hunted, when all the
waters are polluted, when all the air is unsafe to
breathe, only then will you discover you cannot
eat money."

—Cree Tribe prophecy

"And yet—and yet—one's kite will rise on the
wind as far as ever one has string to let it go. It
tugs and tugs and will go, and one is glad the
further it goes, even if everybody else is nasty
about it."

—D. H. Lawrence

 "Open the window of your mind. Allow the
fresh air, new lights and new truths to enter."

—Amit Ray

"If you wish to know the divine, feel the wind on
your face and a warm sun on your hand."

—Buddha

"Love, free as air, at sight of human ties,
Spreads his light wings, and in a moment flies."

—Alexander Pope

"A cloud does not know why it moves in just
such a direction and at such a speed, it feels an
impulse…this is the place to go now. But the
sky knows the reason and the patterns behind
all clouds, and you will know, too, when you lift
yourself high enough to see beyond horizons."

—Richard Bach

"There are some things you learn best in calm,
and some in storm."
  —Willa Cather

"There is a saying in the Neverland that, every
time you breathe, a grown-up dies."
  —J. M. Barrie from *Peter Pan*

"Let's go fly a kite
Up to the highest height
Let's go fly a kite and send it soaring
Up through the atmosphere
Up where the air is clear
Oh let's go fly a kite."
  —Robert B. Sherman and Richard M. Sherman

"We cannot direct the wind, but we can adjust
the sails."
  —Dolly Parton

"The pessimist complains about the wind; the optimist expects it to change; the realist adjusts the sails."

—William Arthur Ward

"A sailor is an artist whose medium is the wind. But now I feel the wind more sensitively than ever before. It touches my face, blows over my skin, enters my body, more essential than blood. At this moment I want for nothing. I am whole, complete, one, transcendent."

—Webb Chiles

"Your head is humming and it won't go,
    in case you don't know
The piper's calling you to join him
Dear lady, can you hear the wind blow,
    and did you know
Your stairway lies on the whispering wind."

—Led Zeppelin

"Close your eyes and turn your face into
the wind. Feel it sweep in an invisible ocean
of exultation. Suddenly, you know you are
alive."

　—Vera Nazarian

"Absence weakens mediocre passions and
increases great ones, as the wind blows out
candles and kindles fires."

　—François de la Rochefoucauld

"And forget not that the earth delights to feel
your bare feet and the winds long to play with
your hair."

　—Khalil Gibran

"To a crazy ship all winds are contrary."

　—George Herbert

"When everything seems to be going against you, remember that the airplane takes off against the wind, not with it."

—Henry Ford

"Notice that the stiffest tree is most easily cracked, while the bamboo or willow survives by bending with the wind."

—Bruce Lee

"It was one of those March days when the sun shines hot and the wind blows cold: when it is summer in the light, and winter in the shade."

—Charles Dickens

"Do not worry if you have built your castles in the air. They are where they should be. Now put the foundations under them."

—Henry David Thoreau

"Flower petals in the breeze look like a butterfly flapping its wings. My love for you takes flight like a white orchid blushing pink."

—Jarod Kintz

"For breath is life, and if you breathe well you will live long on earth."

—Sanskrit proverb

"Wind warns
 November's done with.
The blown leaves make bat-shapes,
Web-winged and furious."

—Sylvia Plath

"Gliders, sailplanes, they are wonderful flying machines. It's the closest you can come to being a bird."

—Neil Armstrong

"You know that our breathing is the inhaling and exhaling of air. The organ that serves for this is the lungs that lie round the heart, so that the air passing through them thereby envelops the heart. Thus breathing is a natural way to the heart. And so, having collected your mind within you, lead it into the channel of breathing through which air reaches the heart and, together with this inhaled air, force your mind to descend into the heart and remain there."

—Nicephorus the Solitary

"The path of humanity is always coordinated with heaven and earth in the alternation of movement and stillness. Human energy is always in communion with heaven and earth in the alternation of exhalation and inhalation."

—Thomas Cleary

"Four elements, Hydrogen, carbon, oxygen
and nitrogen, also provide an example of the
astonishing togetherness of our universe. They
make up the 'organic' molecules that constitute
living organisms on the planet, and the nuclei of
these same elements interact to generate the light
of its star. Then the organisms on the planet come
to depend wholly on that starlight, as they must
if life is to persist. So it is that all life on the Earth
runs on sunlight."

—George Walk

"It is not so much for its beauty that the forest
makes a claim upon men's hearts, as for that
subtle something, that quality of air that
emanation from old trees, that so wonderfully
changes and renews a weary spirit."

—Robert Louis Stevenson

"The finest workers in stone are not copper or steel tools, but the gentle touches of air and water working at their leisure with a liberal allowance of time."

—Henry David Thoreau

"The older you get the stronger the wind gets— and it's always in your face."

—Pablo Picasso

"I fly because it releases my mind from the tyranny of petty things…"

—Antoine de Saint-Exupéry